5

"I read signs,"
Says Peter Malone.
"I know how to read them
By myself alone.
I like to see
What they have to say.
It makes a game
That's fun to play."

"Then mail this present
    To Grandma Malone.
She'll be glad to know
    How smart you have grown.

3

Just watch the signs
    For the name of the street.
And here's some money
    For buying a treat."

"Mamma, don't worry.
    Our number is three.
The names of the streets
    Are easy to see."

PLEASE
DON'T
PARK
HERE!
ELLA MALONE
HILL STREET
IDA, NEW YORK
TUFFY

"We won't get lost
   Or have to holler.
Here, Tuffy, your sign's
   Right on your collar."

Jaw Breakers 1¢ ?

Candy Lips 2¢ ?

Licorice Whips 2¢ ?

Bubble Gum Cigars 10¢ ?

Red Hot Dollars 1¢ ?

Cones 10¢ ?

Candy Buttons 5¢ ?

Nonpareils 1¢ ?

Gum Drops 5 for 1¢ ?

Maple Sugar 5¢ ?

Candy Bananas 2 for 5¢ ?

All Day Suckers 15¢ ?

THIS CLOCK IS ALWAYS RIGHT

BE Wise MAIL EARLY

AIR MAIL AND SPECIAL DELIVERY

LOCAL MAIL

PAPERS AND PACKAGES

OUT OF TOWN

PARCEL POST

JOIN THE AIR FORCE

SEE THE MOON

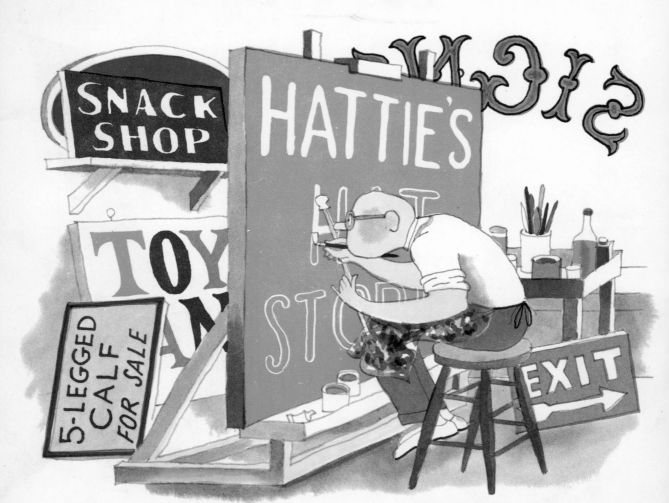

BEWARE of the DOG
NO SMOKING PLEASE
'S BAKERY
Happy Holiday
MOTEL
HOT DOGS

So here in his play room
Is Peter Malone.
"I've a sign shop," he says,
"All of my own!"

HANDS OFF
PLEASE
DON'T BEWAR
OF MY
DOG
TUFFY
DO NOT
TOUCH
ANYTHING
MALONE
SIGN
SHOP
KEEPOFF
BEETS
IRIS
SEEDS
FOR
BIRDS
LETTUCES